IMAGES
of Sport

BIRMINGHAM CITY
FOOTBALL CLUB

The club's first captain was Billy Edmunds, born locally in nearby Bordesley Green, who led the side to victory over such clubs as Saltley College, Walsall Swifts (the forerunners of Walsall of today), Redditch, Nechells, Harborne, Heathfield (Handsworth), the Lion Works and the Arcadians. A versatile footballer, able to occupy a variety of positions, Edmunds once scored a hat-trick in five minutes…albeit with two goals for Blues and one for the opposition. He became Blues' first honorary secretary and, in later years, after retiring from football, was a very respected and highly successful businessman in Birmingham. He died in Birmingham in 1925, aged seventy-one.

IMAGES
of Sport

BIRMINGHAM CITY
FOOTBALL CLUB

Tony Matthews

TEMPUS

First published 2000
Reprinted 2004

Tempus Publishing Limited
The Mill, Brimscombe Port,
Stroud, Gloucestershire, GL5 2QG
www.tempus-publishing.com

British Library Cataloguing in Publication Data.
A catalogue record for this book is available from the British Library.

ISBN 0 7524 1862 9

Typesetting and origination by Tempus Publishing Limited.
Printed in Great Britain.

Contents

Birmingham City team group, 1955/56. From left to right, back row: Trevor Smith, Gil Merrick, Jackie Lane, Roy Warhurst, Ken Green. Front row: Gordon Astall, Jeff Hall, Len Boyd, Peter Murphy, Alex Govan, Noel Kinsey.

Acknowledgements

There are so many people I would like to thank for assisting me in the compilation of this book…to mention them all would take an extra page, or even two. However, I must acknowledge the following who, perhaps unknowing to them, have helped me a great deal – Ivan Barnsley, David Drage, Dafydd Williams and Roger Baker.

There are also some fellow football statisticians who have assisted in some way, namely Ray Spiller, Jim Creasey, Ron Hockings, Mike Davage, Wade Martin, Peter Wyatt, Colin Mackenzie, John Hendley and Robert Bradley (none of whom support the Blues I might add) and also I have to thank the handful of authors, newspaper reporters, sports columnists and such likes up and down the country whose work I have thumbed through to check out various facts and figures in relation to players and matches. Then there are the former Blues stars, including my good friend Ambrose 'Jock' Mulraney, who have also helped simply because they played for the club. I must also thank my wife, Margaret, for putting up with my moodiness when things haven't gone according to plan on the computer.

Last but by no means least I must not forget Birmingham City Football Club itself and the people within St Andrew's – if there hadn't been a soccer team then obviously there wouldn't have been a book.

Introduction

The West Midlands is one of the cradles of professional football – certainly in England – and has always been rich in soccer folklore with Aston Villa, West Bromwich Albion and Wolverhampton Wanderers dominating the game for long periods. The first two were dominant in both League and Cup competitions between 1887 and 1920 and the latter a forceful outfit during the 1950s. In contrast, Birmingham City have not always found it easy to exist or indeed grab the headlines with those three clubs doing so well and, consequently, over the years the Blues have won very few honours. Formed in 1875 as Small Heath Alliance and founder members of the Second Division of the Football League in 1892, the Blues have never won the Football League championship or carried off the FA Cup. Yet the St Andrew's club has its own special place in soccer history.

They have tasted success in the League Cup and were the first British club side to play in a major European final, losing to Barcelona in the 1960 Inter Cities Fairs Cup. They have also won twice and lost twice at Wembley in FA Cup finals. Back in 1888 they were the first club to be formed into a limited company and a little over ninety years later transferred the first £1 million player, Trevor Francis, to Nottingham Forest. Besides Francis, many more great players have proudly worn the famous blue shirts of Birmingham City, among them are: Scottish international Bertie Auld, 1931 FA Cup final skipper Ned Barkas, long-serving Malcolm Beard, 1956 FA Cup final captain Len Boyd, goalscorer supreme Joe Bradford, the versatile Kenny Burns, inside forward Johnny Crosbie, forties star Don Dearson, full-backs Ken Green and Jeff Hall, 'Happy' Harry Hampton, forties hero Fred Harris, England goalkeeper Harry Hibbs, Welshman Caesar Jenkyns, play anywhere Dennis Jennings, centre forward Charlie Wilson Jones, wing-half Howard Kendall, the Latchford brothers (Bob and Dave), Alec Leake, George Liddell, Gil Merrick (another England goalkeeper), Peter 'Spud' Murphy, Billy Ollis from the 1890s, Welsh international Malcolm Page, South African Ted Purdon, centre half Trevor Smith, centre forward-cum-defender Cyril Trigg, Frank Worthington and Ron Wylie. Blues have also had some excellent managers including Leslie Knighton, Harry Storer, Arthur Turner, Stan Cullis, Sir Alf Ramsey, Ron Saunders, Dave Mackay, Jim Smith, Lou Macari and current boss Trevor Francis.

There have been good times when Blues' supporters have celebrated by singing that traditional battle hymn *Keep Right on to the End of the Road* – which has reverberated around St Andrew's and elsewhere, including Wembley. There have also been bad times, with relegations and humiliating defeats against non-League opposition, but the club has carried on regardless, looking – sooner rather than later one hopes – to join the elite in the Premiership and so brush shoulders once more with the top teams of English football. Nothing else would please the ardent fans at St Andrew's more than to meet up again with city rivals Aston Villa and beat them in the top flight of English football!

Roll Of Honour

League Division Two champions:
1892/93, 1920/21, 1947/48, 1954/55

League Division Two runners-up:
1893/94, 1900/01, 1902/03, 1971/72, 1984/85

League Division Three (now Division Two) champions:
1994/95

League Division Three runners-up:
1991/92

Football League Cup winners:
1962/63

FA Cup runners-up:
1930/31, 1955/56

Inter Cities Fairs Cup runners-up:
1958/60, 1960/61

Leyland Daf Trophy winners:
1990/91

Auto Windscreen Shield winners:
1994/95

FA Youth Cup runners-up:
1966/67

One

The Dawn of a
New Club

Blues line-up, c. 1882. The club was founded in 1875 as Small Heath Alliance by an enthusiastic group of cricketers who wanted something to do in the winter months. Using wasteland in Arthur Street (Small Heath), their first match was a friendly against Holte Wanderers (Aston), which ended in a 1-1 draw. They fielded the following team: Will Edden (goalkeeper), his brothers George and Tom, Arthur Wright, Fred and Tom James, Billy Edmunds, David Keys, Charlie Barmore, Clifford Barr and Jack Sparrow. Keys was the scorer of the first-ever Blues' goal. Muntz Street became Blues' home ground in 1877 and, during the first campaign conducted from it, the team went twenty-two games without defeat. Paying a yearly rent of £5 to use Muntz Street, Blues were to stay there for twenty-nine years until 1906, when they moved to St Andrew's. In 1881, six years after their formation, Blues entered the FA Cup for the first time, beating Derby Town 4-1 before losing in the next round 6-0 to Wednesbury Old Athletic. Over the next three years several players came and left the club and results were indifferent, but a bright future was in store.

Harry Morris, an apprentice plumber, gained a place in Blues' first team at the age of eighteen in 1884/85. Few men have done more for Blues than Morris, for it was he who eventually 'found' the St Andrew's ground. He had become a director of the club in 1903 and his two sons followed him onto the Blues' board. Born in Birmingham in April 1866, he was a very shrewd businessman and was one of the first people to see the potential in talking pictures. At the time of his death in 1931 – two months after Blues had appeared in their first FA Cup final – he was a director of several local cinemas in the city of Birmingham.

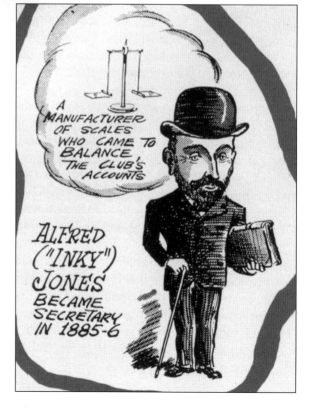

In the mid-1880s, Birmingham-born Alfred 'Inky' Jones, a scales manufacturer by trade, was appointed the first 'official' secretary of Blues and in the 1885/86 season he saw the team reach the semi-final of the FA (English) Cup, only to lose 4-0 to neighbours West Bromwich Albion. Blues' share of the gate receipts from that encounter amounted to a misely £4 5s and Jones, who also looked after the club's accounts, was not too pleased with that return.

Blues became founder members of the Football League Division Two in 1892/93 and won the championship at the first attempt, although surprisingly did not win promotion (losing to Newton Heath – now Manchester United – in the test matches). In December 1892, in front of just 2,000 spectators, Blues whipped Darwen 12-0 at home to register their biggest League victory which still stands today, although they equalled it with an identical scoreline against Doncaster Rovers in April 1903. Despite their disappointment at missing out on promotion, Blues battled on and the following season (1893/94) they clinched runners-up spot in the Second Division and claimed their rightful place in the top flight. This photograph was probably taken prior to the first home game of the 1893/94 season against Rotherham Town (a 4-3 win). The players are, from left to right, back row: Edwin Jolley, George Hollis, Edwin Devey. Seated: Jack Hallam, Bernard Pumphrey, Frank Mobley, Caeser Jenkyns, Freddie Wheldon and Tommy Hands. On ground: Billy Ollis and Jack Lee. Directly behind the shield, in his black shorts, is giant 6ft 5in goalkeeper George Hollis – one of the tallest players ever to serve the Blues. Welshman Caeser Jenkyns, a resolute defender, scored 13 goals in 99 senior appearances for Blues between 1888 and 1895. He was transferred to Woolwich Arsenal and won a total of eight caps for his country.

In April 1891 Blues signed Billy Ollis from Warwick County. A solid, industrious right-half, born within walking distance of the club's ground, he went on to make 112 senior appearances for the club and took over the captaincy of the team from Caeser Jenkyns. Ollis moved to Hereford Thistle in 1896 and retired through injury three years later. He was significant in helping the Blues win the Second Division title and promotion in successive seasons.

Playing in the same team as Ollis was defender Alec Leake, born in Small Heath, who was recruited from Old Hill Wanderers in 1894. The joker in the pack, he played in more than 220 games for Blues up to 1902, when he moved across the city to sign for rivals Aston Villa. A classy footballer, Leake played for England five times and won an FA Cup winners medal in 1905. He also lined up for Burnley and later became trainer of Crystal Palace (1912-15), Merthyr Town and Walsall (1922-33). During the 1930s he coached at various schools all over Great Britain. Leake was actually chosen as reserve for England at the age of forty-one.

Arthur Archer – born in Derby – was one of Blues' first recognized full-backs. A determined, forceful player who was very imposing, he served the club for five years, from 1897 to 1902, during which time he appeared in 170 first team matches. A big pal of centre half Alec Leake, they both helped Blues to runners-up spot in the Second Division in 1901. Archer also played for Queen's Park Rangers, Brighton & Hove Albion, Norwich City and Millwall. He died during the Second World War.

In April 1905 Blues met Stoke in a First Division fixture at Muntz Street but, sadly for the home supporters in the 10,000 crowd (around 4,000 below the seasonal average incidentally), the visitors won by a goal to nil. This photograph shows Stoke defending a Blues corner-kick from the right.

Blues playing in a League game against Wolverhampton Wanderers (who are wearing the dark shorts) at Molineux on 15 October 1904. A crowd of 8,000 saw Harry Wilcox score the only goal to give Blues a 1-0 victory.

In September 1905, a crowd of 15,000 saw Blues beat Sheffield United 2-0 at Muntz Street in a First Division match. Once again Harry Wilcox featured on the scoresheet along with Arthur 'Pecker' Mounteney. In this picture Blues are under pressure as the Blades attack in force.

Two
New Ground, New Era

The Blues 1905 team line-up.

Blues moved to their present ground at St Andrew's in December 1906 and in their last season at Muntz Street they finished seventh in Division Two and reached the fourth round of the FA Cup. Their best League win in 1905/06 was a 7-0 home success over Middlesbrough when Benny Green struck five goals. Nottingham Forest were thrashed 5-0 away and Sheffield Wednesday 5-1 at home. Blues' heaviest defeat in the League saw them go down 5-0 at Woolwich Arsenal. This is the Blues line-up at the start of the 1905/06 campaign. From left to right, back row: Simms (assistant trainer), Norman (trainer), Glover, Robinson, W. Adams (club president), Stokes, Howard, Dougherty, Dr Stanley (director), Alfred Jones (secretary). Front row: Beer, Green, Mounteney, Wigmore, Jones, Wilcox, Field. Tickle (featured on the postcard on the previous page) was absent when the photograph was taken. The three trophies (all won in the previous season) are The Lord Mayor of Birmingham Charity Cup, the Birmingham Senior Cup and the Staffordshire Senior Cup.

A badge of the period featuring the club.

England international inside forward Jimmy Windridge, who was born in Small Heath, had two spells with Birmingham. He first joined the club as a junior in 1898, turned professional three years later and transferred to Chelsea for £190 in 1905. After spending six years at Stamford Bridge (scoring 58 goals in 152 games for the Londoners) he then signed for Middlesbrough before returning to Blues in 1914. He retired during the First World War after netting a total of 19 goals in 61 appearances for the club. He won eight caps for his country and claimed seven goals (1908-09). During the war, Windridge organized a scratch Blues team to play in local Charity matches. He was also a fine cricketer with Warwickshire.

Chunky Yorkshire-born inside forward Benny Green had the honour of scoring the first goal at St Andrew's – for Blues against Preston North End in a Division One League game in December 1906. He joined the club from Barnsley in October 1903 and stayed with Blues for six years before transferring to Burnley. He had a fine record as a goalscorer for Blues, netting 46 times in almost 200 senior appearances. After Burnley he had spells with Preston North End and Blackpool prior to announcing his retirement in 1917. Unfortunately, Green had a reputation of being a trouble-maker – not only for defenders.

Amateur goalkeeper Herbert Crossthwaite was a Lancastrian, born in Preston, who played for Blackpool, Fulham and Exeter City before joining Blues in December 1910. He made 49 appearances for the club between the posts up until 1914, when he moved to Stoke. He retired in 1915 to concentrate on being a police constable in the City of Birmingham. He rose to the rank of inspector and was instrumental in organising sporting events within the police force. His brother played for Stockport County.

Centre half Alex McClure played for five major Midland sides during a fine career which spanned fifteen years. Born in Workington in 1892 he joined Blues in 1912 and scored four goals in 198 outings for the club before leaving to sign for Aston Villa in December 1923. He switched to Stoke ten months later and then served with Coventry City and Walsall before retiring to become a coach with Luton Town in 1927, a position he later assumed back at St Andrew's where he also acted as assistant manager. A member of Blues' Second Division championship winning side in 1921, McClure represented the Football League. He died in 1973.

In 1912/13, Blues finished third in the Second Division of the Football League – missing promotion to the top flight by just four points (Preston North End and Burnley went up as champions and runners-up respectively). Blues lost both their League games against Preston and the away match at Burnley, having earlier beaten the runners-up elect 3-0 at St Andrew's. This photograph shows the full squad of Blues players (and the club's directors) under manager Bob McRoberts, a former player himself who is seen standing third from the left in the second row down. He has Billy George, the former Aston Villa and England goalkeeper, who was Blues' trainer at this time, to his right.

Richard Gibson was a flying winger with a fiery temper. Born in London in 1889, he joined Blues at the age of twenty-two and went on to score 19 goals in 120 first team appearances before transferring to Manchester United in 1921. Unfortunately, Gibson often over-elaborated when in possession and on many occasions came under the wrath of the home supporters for being 'too fancy'.

Having just missed promotion to the top flight in 1919/20, Blues went on to win the Second Division championship the following season, pipping Cardiff City on goal-average, with Bristol City third and Blackpool fourth. Pictured here is the Birmingham FC squad of 1921/22 with chairman, directors and staff. From left to right, back row: W. Kendrick (assistant trainer), Neil, Sharp, Getgood, Reddington, Tremelling, Hunter, Liddell, Jenkins, Brown, S. Scholey (masseur), Eccles (trainer). Second row: F.H. Richards (secretary), Burkinshaw, J. Harris (director), Roulson, H. Cant (chairman), W. Hart (director), T. Turley (director), White, H.S. Thomas (director), S. Richards (assistant secretary). Third row: Booth, Whitehouse, Hampton, McClure, Womack (captain), Barton, Elkes, Lane, Jones, Davies, Harvey. On ground: Cameron, Dixon, Crosbie, Linley, Bradford, Daws. The three trophies are the Birmingham Cup, the Second Division championship shield and the Lord Mayor of Birmingham Charity Cup. Unfortunately, things didn't turn out as planned in the First Division and Blues had to battle hard and long before finally holding on to their top sector status by claiming eighteenth place, only five points away from relegation. They lost ten games at St Andrew's (the worst home record in the division) and accumulated a mere 37 points out of a possible 84.

After the First World War, Blues had Dan Tremelling in goal. Known as the 'India Rubber Man', he had started his career as a full-back and joined Blues from Lincoln City in 1919, having become a very fine custodian with the Imps. Brave and reliable, he went on to play in 395 games for Blues, helping them win the Second Division championship in 1921. He also gained one England cap and represented the Football League on three occasions. He was replaced between the posts by another great goalkeeper Harry Hibbs. On leaving St Andrew's, Tremelling joined Bury in 1932 and later returned to Birmingham as Blues' assistant trainer from 1936 until 1941. In 1924 Tremelling had dramatically saved a penalty taken by Cardiff City's Len Davies in the final League game of that season which prevented the Welsh side from winning the title. He had joined Blues on the thirteenth of the month, left the club on the thirteenth and spent thirteen years at St Andrew's, but the number wasn't at all unlucky for the big fellow as his career statistics clearly indicate. On retiring Tremelling became landlord of the Old Lodge near the Blues' ground. His brother Bill played for Blackpool and Preston.

When Blues won the Second Division title in 1920/21 one of the star players was outside right Laurie Burkinshaw who scored six goals – and made many more – in 35 League appearances. A Yorkshireman, he signed for Blues in August 1919 having earlier assisted Sheffield Wednesday and Rotherham. He went on to net 12 goals in 75 outings for the club before transferring to Halifax Town in June 1922. His brother Jack also played for Sheffield Wednesday.

Jack Jones was a formidable full-back, as tough as they come, strong, robust, determined, competitive and built like an ox. A Yorkshireman from Rotherham, he joined Blues for £2,000 in August 1920 from Sunderland and formed a fine partnership with Frank Womack. He helped Blues win the Second Division title in 1921 and went on to make 237 appearances for the club before moving to Nelson in 1927. He represented the Football League XI on one occasion, but deserved a lot more honours than he received. He never shirked a tackle, always giving 110 per cent on the field and it was known for him to have injections before a game to 'ease the pain'.

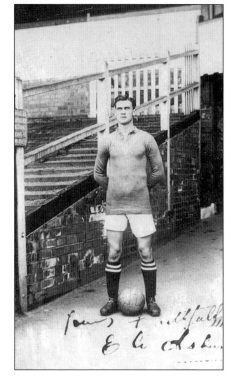

Tough-tackling full-back Elias Ashurst made 70 first team appearances for Blues over a four-year period from 1922 to 1926. Born in the north-east of England, he joined the club from Stanley United but was forced to retire prematurely at the age of twenty-four owing to a mysterious illness. Sadly, he died in his home town of Willington a year later in December 1927. Elias' brother Billy, also a full-back, played for Notts County, West Bromwich Albion and England.

After scoring 242 goals in 376 games for arch-rivals Aston Villa, centre forward Harry Hampton (pictured left), who was nicknamed 'Appy', joined Blues at the age of thirty-four in February 1920. The former idol of Villa Park, who won two FA Cup winners' medals, a League championship medal and four England caps while with Villa, quickly helped Blues win the Second Division title. He stayed at St Andrew's until September 1922 when he moved to Newport County. Scotsman Johnny Crosbie from Glasgow played alongside Hampton in Blues' forward line in that 1920/21 championship-winning season. Crosbie cost the club a record £3,700 when signed from Ayr United in May 1920. He became a big hit with the St Andrew's faithful and went on to score 72 goals in 432 appearances for Blues, helping them reach the 1931 FA Cup final. He played twice for Scotland and also starred in one Victory international for his country. He left Blues for Chesterfield in 1932.

Scorer of 13 goals in 85 games for Blues between 1926 and 1932, Wolverhampton-born winger Benny Bond suffered with knee injuries during his time at St Andrew's. He was a fast and tricky player who was forced to retire at the age of twenty-seven.

Outside left Ted Liney was a knock-kneed, balding miner before engaging himself in serious football with his local club Worksop Town. He joined Blues in December 1920 and was a valuable member of their Second Division championship-winning team in his first season with the club. He went on to play 118 times for Blues, scoring eleven goals, before transferring to Nottingham Forest in 1926. He later played for Mansfield Town after a brief spell with non-League Sutton.

Three
Bradford, Hibbs and the Thirties

The two captains, Tommy Glidden (Albion) and Ned Barkas (Blues) shake hands before the 1931 FA Cup final at Wembley. The referee is Mr W.H. Kingscott.

Blues' champion goalscorer of all-time is Joe Bradford, who spent over sixteen years at St Andrew's. He first joined the club in February 1920 and retired in May 1936. Born in a Leicestershire village on 22 January 1901, the day Queen Victoria died, he once scored 14 goals in one game for his home town club Peggs Green and in 1915/16 he netted 65 goals in total. This record sparked off a surge of interest from League clubs and it was Blues who secured his signature for just £125. Bradford went on to net 267 goals in 445 games for Blues, helping them reach the 1931 FA Cup final. He also won 12 full England caps and represented the Football League on five occasions. He grabbed Blues' equalising goal against West Bromwich Albion in the all-Midlands FA Cup final of 1931 and, during the 1920s and early '30s, was one of the finest marksmen in the game. In fact, he was the club's top-scorer (or joint top-scorer) every season from 1921 to 1933. He was given an emotional send-off from St Andrew's when he was transferred to Bristol City in May 1935. Joe's brother, William Bradford, played for Walsall and his cousin, Hugh Adcock, starred for Leicester City and England. In fact, both Joe and Hugh lined up in their country's forward line in three full internationals against France, Spain and Ireland in 1929. Bradford became a licensee after retiring and died in September 1980, aged seventy-nine.

LEWIS STOKER.

Right half Lew Stoker appeared in 246 League and Cup games for Blues over a period of eight years from 1930 to 1938. He won three England caps and represented the Football League during his time at St Andrew's when he lined up across the middle of the park with the likes of George Morrall, Tom Fillingham, Charlie Calladine, Joe Loughran and Jack Sykes. An excellent 'feeder of the attack', Stoker played for Nottingham Forest after leaving Blues and retired during the Second World War.

One of the finest goalscoring wingers in Blues' pre-war days, George Briggs secured a goal every three games for the club, netting 107 times in 324 League and Cup appearances. A darting outside right born in Yorkshire, he joined the club for £400 with Aubrey Scriven from Denaby United in December 1923 and remained at St Andrew's for ten years before transferring to Plymouth Argyle. Briggs lined up for Blues in the 1931 FA Cup final. His brother-in-law Fred Tunstall played for Sheffield United.

Blues players training at Bushey Park prior to their 1931 FA Cup final showdown with neighbours West Bromwich Albion. The players are, from left to right: Curtis, Crosbie, Fillingham, Gregg, Stoker, Hibbs, Firth, Randle, Morrell, Leslie. The fellow in the background with the flat cap is trainer Archie Taylor.

JAMES A. CRINGAN
BIRMINGHAM

Scotsman Jimmy Cringan scored 12 goals in 285 games for Blues between 1922 and 1934. A fine, intelligent, hard-working wing half, he was born in Lanarkshire in 1904 and had trials with Sunderland and Bury before moving to St Andrew's. When he left Blues he took over as player-manager of Boston United. He was a 'bostin' footballer and played for Blues in the 1931 FA Cup final.

Blues visited Wembley Stadium for the first time in April 1931. After knocking out Liverpool, Port Vale, Watford, Chelsea and Sunderland, they took on neighbours West Bromwich Albion in the FA Cup final. However, on a rain-soaked afternoon in front of 90,368 spectators they went down 2-1 to the Baggies. The scoreline may well have been different had a smartly headed 'goal' from Bob Gregg not been ruled out for offside. The linesman's flag went in favour of the Baggies and perhaps denied Blues of glory. Joe Bradford scored Blues' goal that day while 'W.G.' Richardson netted both for Albion. *Above:* The fans enter the stadium prior to kick-off. *Right:* Blues' goalkeeper Harry Hibbs punches clear as Albion push forward during the second half.

This is Blues' Wembley squad from 1931. Left to right, back row: Johnny Crosbie, George Morrall, Harry Hibbs, Alec Leslie, Ernie Curtis. Front row: Jimmy Cringan, George Briggs, Joe Bradford, Ned Barkas, Jack Firth (reserve), Bob Gregg. On ground: George Liddell and Bill Horsman (reserve).

Full-back George Liddell made almost 350 appearances for Blues between 1920 and 1932. A former Rugby League player born in Durham, he played in the 1931 FA Cup final and replaced Frank Womack in the full-back position at St Andrew's. A small, dapper, moustached defender, he was a teacher by profession (teaching at schools in Cotteridge and Washwood Heath) and often missed Blues' mid-week fixtures. On retiring Liddell became manager at St Andrew's from 1933 until 1939.

One of Blues' greatest goalkeepers, Harry Hibbs made 389 first team appearances for the club (only Gil Merrick and Dan Tremelling have more between the posts), won 25 England caps, represented the Football League three times and toured South Africa with the FA party. This showed that he was one of the best 'keepers in the country during the 1929-36 period. Born in Wilnecote near Tamworth, he joined the playing staff at St Andrew's in 1924, turned professional the same year and, after replacing Tremelling in the first team, he held his position until retiring in 1940, immediately after appearing in a farewell benefit game against Aston Villa.

Harry Hibbs later managed nearby Walsall from 1944 to 1951, but pulled out of football completely in 1963. Hibbs died in May 1984, four days before his seventy-eighth birthday. His uncle, Hubert Pearson, and cousin, Harold Pearson, both kept goal for West Bromwich Albion and in fact Harold lined up for the Baggies against the Blues in the 1931 FA Cup final.

31

After beating Blues in the 1931 FA Cup final, West Bromwich Albion went on to clinch promotion back to the First Division. On Christmas Day 1931 the Baggies entertained Blues at The Hawthorns for the first time in a top division game since February 1927 and in front of a 38,000 crowd Blues won the match 1-0 thanks to a goal by outside left Ernie Curtis. Here Blues' goalkeeper Harry Hibbs palms away a long range shot from Albion's outside right and captain Tommy Glidden (not in picture).

Ernie Curtis spent five and a half years at St Andrew's from March 1928 to November 1933. In that time he scored 53 goals in 180 appearances, occupying the left-wing position. Born in Cardiff, he transferred from Ninian Park to Blues for £3,000 and replaced Billy Ellis in the first team. Capped three times by Wales, Curtis rejoined Cardiff City on leaving St Andrew's and after playing for Coventry City and Hartlepool United he went back to Ninian Park for a third time as an assistant-coach. He was eighty-five when he died in November 1992.

A twentieth minute strike by inside left Fred Harris on his senior debut for Blues earned his side a 2-1 home victory over rivals Aston Villa in the First Division derby at St Andrew's on 25 August 1934. Harris (pictured right, turning away from goal) drove the ball home after some smart work on the right by Dave Mangnall. A crowd of 54,200 saw outside left Billy Guest win the contest for Blues with a second goal after 'Pongo' Waring had netted for Villa.

Blues' skipper Fred Harris shakes hands with Tommy Lawton, captain of Notts County, before the start of a third round FA Cup-tie between the teams at St Andrew's in January 1948. County won the game 2-0 in front of 53,000 spectators.

Between February 1934 and March 1935 Dave Mangnall partnered Joe Bradford in Blues' attack and for a time the pairing looked very dangerous. But Mangnall, from Wigan, suffered with injuries which resulted in him leaving the club for West Ham United. Signed from Huddersfield, he entered top-grade soccer with Leeds United and during a fine career which spanned over twenty-five years as a player and manager, he could well have visited every soccer ground in the country. He scored 15 goals in 39 games for Blues and in League football netted well over 120 goals in less than 200 outings. He once scored ten times in a reserve team game for Leeds and then hit 42 goals for Huddersfield in 1931/32 but was dropped. Mangnall quit football in 1952 and went into business in Cornwall.

During the 1930s one of Blues' finest servants was another ex-Huddersfield Town player, defender Ned Barkas. He joined the ranks at St Andrew's for £4,000 from the Yorkshire club in 1928 and over the next nine years amassed 288 senior appearances and scored 9 goals. He left Blues for Chelsea in May 1937, linking up with his former manager Leslie Knighton. He later returned to the Midlands to become player-manager of Solihull Town and during the Second World War worked as a chargehand. He died in 1962, aged sixty-one.

Blues' goalkeeper Harry Hibbs punches clear during his side's 2-0 defeat against Stoke City at The Victoria Ground in September 1934. The following season the Potters came to St Andrew's and belted Blues 5-0 and in the last season before the war (1938/39) they again hammered Blues 6-3 at home. Over a period of six years from 1933 to 1939 Blues met Stoke City twelve times in the First Division and did not won once.

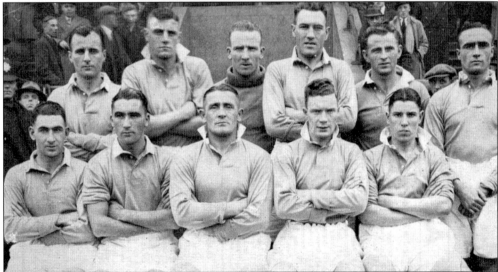

Blues' line-up at the start of the 1935/36 season in Division One. Left to right, back row: Stoker, Grosvenor, Hibbs, Fillingham, Steele, Loughran. Front row: White, Harris, Barkas, Jones, Guest. Blues finished twelfth in the table and went out of the FA Cup in the third round to Barnsley. Fred Harris was the only ever-present in the side and Blues' top scorer was Wilson Jones with 20 goals in League and Cup. Blues best win of the season was a 4-0 home triumph over Portsmouth and the average League attendance at St Andrew's was almost 23,000.

In September 1936 a crowd of 26,013 saw West Bromwich Albion beat Blues 3-2 in a First Division match at The Hawthorns. Here Blues' defender Jack Sykes gets in front of Teddy Sandford to head the ball clear as Albion threaten the Brummie Road end goal. Lew Stoker is the Blues player on the right.

The Blues' matchday programme for season 1935/36 and 1936/37 would cost the avid supporter just 2d (1p). Each comprised 12 pages and there were approximately 5,000 printed for each home match. Both these issues shown here were for home League games against Stoke City. The 1935/36 game saw the Potters win 5-0 in front of 15,000 fans and the following season six goals were scored, but only two by Blues, who went down 4-2 before 10,000 spectators.

Again it's action from a local derby between Blues and West Bromwich Albion as Don Dearson finds the net and the Baggies are beaten 2-1 at St Andrew's on 15 April 1938. This defeat helped send the Baggies down into the Second Division.

A Welshman, born near Wrexham, Charlie Wilson Jones scored 71 goals in 151 senior appearances for Blues and added another 45 in 75 wartime games. A fine centre forward, brave, energetic, confident yet frail-looking, this redhead certainly knew where the goal frame was and for thirteen years gave the St Andrew's faithful plenty to cheer about. He joined Blues from Wrexham in September 1934, having earlier had trials with Bolton Wanderers, and he left the club for Nottingham Forest in September 1947. Capped twice by Wales, he helped Blues win the transitional Football League (South) championship in 1945/46.

Born in the same county as another great Blues' goalscorer Joe Bradford, Cyril Trigg actually began his playing career as a full-back. However, he developed into a highly effective marksman who went on to score 160 goals in almost 400 games for Blues in League, FA Cup and wartime football. He joined the club as a professional in 1935 and left in 1954 to become player-coach of Stourbridge. He helped Blues win the League (South) title in 1946 and the Second Division championship two years later. As hard as nails, he feared no one and during the war served with the RAF in India and Burma.

Four
Wartime
Football

Like most other clubs, Blues played only three League games at the start of the ill-fated 1939/40 season before the Second World War broke out. One of Blues' Second Division encounters was a home clash with Burnley. Here, Don Dearson fires Blues ahead in their 2-0 win on 2 September. This game, along with others, was later declared null and void.

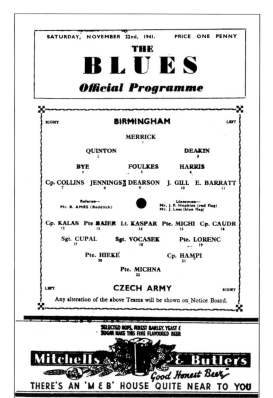

In November 1941 the Czech Army side played Blues at St Andrew's in a prestigious friendly. Blues won the game comfortably by four goals to nil.

On 5 November 1945 Blues flew out to West Germany to entertain B.A.O.R. Here, the official party poses for a photograph prior to boarding the aircraft.

Birmingham added the name 'City' to their title during the war – probably in 1943 – and one of the first team groups of the side under that name is shown here. From left to right, back row: Sid Owen, Ted Duckhouse, Gil Merrick, Dave Massart, Fred Harris. Front row: Jock Mulraney, Neil Dougall, Dennis Jennings, Arthur Turner, Harold Bodle, George Edwards.

Centre half Arthur Turner played for Stoke City before joining Blues in January 1939. Unfortunately, the war interrupted his duties at St Andrew's but he still managed to play in almost 240 games, 186 during the hostilities. He left the club for Southport in 1948 and after managing Crewe Alexandra and acting as assistant-boss at his former club Stoke, he returned to take charge of Blues in November 1954. He quickly guided the team to promotion from the Second Division and then took them to the 1956 FA Cup final before leaving in 1959 to manage Oxford United.

In 1946, after the fighting in Europe had ended, Blues entertained Sparta Prague in a friendly at St Andrew's and here manager Harry Storer introduces his players to the Lord Mayor of Birmingham prior to kick off.

During the Second World War, fighter planes bombed St Andrew's and for a time Blues had to use neighbouring Villa Park and Leamington Spa's pitch to play their home matches. Early in 1940 St Andrew's was the only Football League ground in the country to be shut down because of the threat of air attacks over the city of Birmingham. After consulting Parliament the ban was lifted after four months. This photograph shows the bomb-battered roof over the spectators on the popular Spion Kop terracing at St Andrew's in 1946/47, before workmen put things right and kept out the elements.

The first 'serious' local derby between Blues and their arch-rivals Aston Villa took place at Villa Park on 12 January 1946 in the Football League South Division. A bumper crowd of 63,820 witnessed the 2-2 draw. A week later the two teams played the return fixture at St Andrew's and this time, watched by 40,000 fans, Blues won 3-1 with Wilson Jones (2) and Jock Mularney on target. This photograph shows the two captains George Cummings (Aston Villa) on the left and Fred Harris (Blues) shaking hands before the start of the confrontation at St Andrew's. Scotsman Mulraney, now eighty-three and resident in Kinver, is one of the oldest former Blues players alive today.

In 1946, after missing out on a second Wembley appearance by losing in the FA Cup semi-final to Derby County in a replay, Blues went on an end of season tour to Sweden. This photograph shows officials and players of Birmingham City lining up in the centre circle prior to kick-off of a game at AIK Stockholm. The players featured are, from left to right: Arthur Turner, Gil Merrick, Ted Duckhouse, Frank Mitchell, Sid Owen (in tracksuit), Cyril Trigg, Fred Harris, Neil Dougall, Harold Bodle, Dennis Jennings, George Edwards, Jock Mulraney.

Centre half Ted Duckhouse was released by West Bromwich Albion in 1938 and Blues quickly snapped him up. He did very well at St Andrew's and went on to make 137 League and FA Cup appearances for the club up to 1950 when he moved to Northampton Town.

This Blues team group was taken on tour in Malmo in 1946. From left to right, back row: Fred Harris, Don Dearson, Arthur Turner, Gil Merrick, Frank Mitchell, Dennis Jennings, Harry Storer (manager). Front row: Jock Mulraney, Neil Dougall, Charlie Wilson Jones, Harold Bodle, George Edwards.

Blues' star forward line for the 1946/47 season featured Jock Mulraney, Neil Dougall, Cyril Trigg, Don Dorman and George Edwards. Dorman scored his first goal for the club in the 2-1 FA Cup win at Fulham on 11 January 1947 and between them these five players netted over 120 goals for Blues in League and Cup action.

In 1947/48 Blues won the Second Division title with 59 points, three more than runners-up Newcastle. They won 22 of their 42 games and lost only 5 (2 at home). A total of 55 goals were scored and only 24 conceded (13 at home, 11 away). Blues' defence was one of the strongest and meanest anywhere in the country with goalkeepers Gil Merrick and Jack Wheeler keeping 24 clean sheets between them. Merrick made almost 700 appearances for Blues during and after the Second World War. He starred in 551 League and Cup games and won 24 England caps, conceding 13 goals in the 2 internationals against the Hungarians in 1953 and 1954. He won League (South) and Second Division championship medals with Blues and appeared in the 1956 FA Cup Final. He retired in 1960 and took over as manager, leading Blues to the Fairs Cup final and then victory over Aston Villa in the 1963 League Cup final. He spent four years in charge and later moved into non-League football with Bromsgrove Rovers. Merrick is now seventy-eight years of age and living in Birmingham. The action picture below shows Merrick diving in the Molineux mud in 1950 to prevent a cross reaching Roy Swinbourne. Blues' defender Ted Duckhouse looks on.

Frank Mitchell was born in Australia in June 1922, but moved to England while still a teenager. In 1942 he joined Coventry City, but failed to impress at Highfield Road and the following year, after guesting for the club, he joined Blues, turning professional immediately. He went on to score 8 goals in 106 appearances for Blues before moving to Chelsea in January 1949, later assisting Watford. A fine left half, he helped Blues win the League (South) title in 1946 and the Second Division championship in 1948. He also played for the FA XI and during the war served in the Royal Navy. Mitchell was also a fine cricketer and played in 17 county matches as a medium pace bowler for Warwickshire. He died in 1984.

On their return to the First Division after winning the Second Division title in season 1947/48, Blues quickly got into the routine of playing local derbies and their opening League game of the 1948/49 campaign took them to nearby Molineux where they met a competent Wolverhampton Wanderers side, managed by Stan Cullis, who was later to become boss at St Andrew's. A crowd of 54,361 saw Blues put on a plucky display, holding Wolves to a 2-2 draw with goals from Harold Bodle and Cyril Trigg. In this photograph Blues' goalkeeper Gil Merrick thwarts Wanderers' centre forward Jesse Pye following a left-wing centre. The other players in the picture are Blues' Dennis Jennings (behind Pye) and Fred Harris (4), and Wolves' Jimmy Dunn (8).

Blues' Don Dorman (right) just misses out on a header during Blues' home League game with Leeds United in February 1948. The goalkeeper is Jim Twomey who conceded five goals as Blues ran riot in front of almost 40,000 fans. The visitors scored once in reply.

All local derbies are passionate affairs, especially for the supporters. None more so perhaps than when Blues meet Aston Villa. In April 1950, with Blues already doomed to relegation, the two Second City clubs did battle against each other in a First Division match at St Andrew's and in front of 26,144 fans shared four goals in a 2-2 draw. Cyril Trigg netted twice for Blues who earlier in the season had drawn 1-1 at Villa Park. This picture shows Billy Goffin of Villa heading wide as he rises to a left-wing centre. The other nearby players in the photograph are, from left to right: Ray Ferris (Blues), Trevor Ford (Villa), Ted Duckhouse (Blues), Dennis Jennings (Blues) and Len Boyd (Blues).

Blues' goalkeeper Gil Merrick snatches the ball away from Johnny Downie, the Manchester United inside right, during the 0-0 First Division draw at St Andrew's in March 1950. Dennis Jennings is the other Blues player in the picture.

The following month Newcastle United visited St Andrew's for another First Division match and in front of a 30,000 crowd they won the contest 2-0 with Ernie Taylor (later to star in Blackpool's 1953 FA Cup final victory) and Tommy Walker. Here, Blues' Scottish-born striker Jimmy Dailey goes close to equalising with a header.

In September 1951 Blues' manager Bob Brocklebank signed burly centre forward Tommy Briggs from Coventry City. A prolific scorer, Briggs netted 22 goals in 50 outings for Blues before moving to Blackburn Rovers in December 1952. In a fine career the Chesterfield-born marksman netted 286 goals in 390 League games including seven in one match for Blackburn against Bristol Rovers in 1955. He also played for Plymouth, Grimsby Town and Glentoran.

St Andrew's could house approximately 58,500 spectators in 1950, around 9,000 less than the record attendance at the ground which was set in February 1939 for the visit of Everton in the fifth round of the FA Cup. That day a crowd of 67,341 witnessed a 2-2 draw, Madden scoring twice for Blues. The mid-week replay at Goodison Park drew another bumper crowd of 64,800 and this time Everton went through 2-1.

In August 1951 once again Leeds United, with John Charles in their forward-line, visited St Andrew's to take on Blues in a Second Division match. This time a moderate crowd of just over 17,000 witnessed a 1-1 draw. This picture shows Blues' goalkeeper Gil Merrick gathering a low cross ahead of the Welsh international striker who was known as the 'Gentle Giant'.

Ron Wylie, later to play for Blues, scored the first League goal of his professional career for Notts County against Birmingham City in a Second Division encounter at Meadow Lane in April 1952. It was a diving header (seen here) which flew past Gil Merrick. In fact, Scotsman Wylie scored four goals in this game as Blues were murdered 5-0 in front of a 24,300 crowd.

Scottish-born right-winger Jackie Stewart made the last of 218 senior appearances for Blues in October 1954 away at Leeds. He joined the club from Raith Rovers in January 1948 and held onto the no. 7 shirt for almost six years, helping Blues win promotion from the Second Division in 1948. He eventually returned to Raith in February 1955 after handing over the position to Gordon Astall. A former miner, he was fast and clever, possessed a fine right foot shot and scored all Blues' goals in a 4-1 home win over Manchester City eight months after moving to St Andrew's.

In season 1954/55 Blues couldn't stop scoring. In their 42 Second Division matches they netted 92 goals, the best for more than 60 years (since netting 103 in only 28 League games in 1893/94 when they won promotion from Division Two). In successive home games Blues struck a total of 16 goals, beating Port Vale 7-2 in late November and then hammering Liverpool 9-1 on 11 December. The picture here shows Peter Murphy heading one of his three goals against Port Vale, who the season before had run away with the Third Division (North) championship and also reached the FA Cup semi-final.

Blues won the Second Division title in 1954/55 by playing some decisive attacking football, but at the end of the day they only went up into the top flight on goal average. They amassed 54 points, the same as fellow contenders Luton Town and Rotherham United but it was Blues' solid defence and exciting attack which took them up. They ended the campaign with 22 wins and 10 draws to their credit from 42 matches. Their record of 92 goals for and 47 against was far better than their two challengers. Here, the players celebrate the championship with a cuppa in the dressing room. Trevor Smith (no. 5) had a fine season, as did 'Spud' Murphy (extreme left).

Manager Arthur Turner (second from left) and players Johnny Newman, Jackie Lane, Bill Bradbury and Gil Merrick celebrate Blues' emphatic 5-1 victory at Doncaster which guaranteed them the Second Division championship and promotion to the First Division in May 1955.

In that blistering 5-1 win at Belle Vue against Doncaster Rovers, centre forward Eddie Brown was in sparkling form and here he scores one of Blues' goals past 'keeper Ken Hardwick and the covering full-back. Over 21,300 fans packed into the ground, with 10,000 of them supporting Blues.

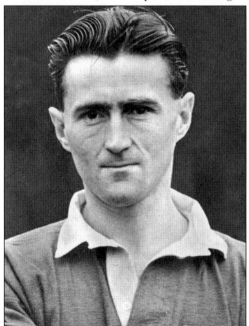

Left: Skipper Len Boyd gave Blues supreme service as a wing-half. Born in London in 1923, he joined the club from Plymouth Argyle in 1945 and made 282 first team appearances, scoring 14 goals, before retiring in 1956. He led Blues to the Second Division championship in 1955 and also at Wembley for the FA Cup final two years later. *Right:* Jeff Hall was a cultured right-back, cool, calm and collected (as they say). He was born in Scunthorpe in 1929 and was an amateur with Bradford Park Avenue before signing for Blues as a professional in 1950 following his national service. He went on to make 264 League and Cup appearances for Blues as well as winning 17 caps for England. Sadly, Hall died of polio in April 1959, aged twenty-nine.

Blues striker Peter Murphy dresses up as Santa Claus to hand out presents at a children's Christmas party in 1955. The other Blues players in the picture are, from left to right: Alex Govan, Eddie Brown and Roy Warhurst.

Blues had appointed former defender Arthur Turner as their manager in November 1954 and within six months he had taken the club into the First Division. Then, almost as quickly, he proudly walked his players down the tunnel and out to the roar of 100,000 fans before the start of the 1956 FA Cup final.

Five

Wembley Blues, Europe and Semi-final Misery

The Blues team of 1955. From left to right, back row: Ray Shaw (trainer), Jeff Hall, Johnny Newman, Trevor Smith, Gil Merrick, Len Boyd, Ken Green, Jack Badham, Dave Fairhurst (physiotherapist). Front row: Gordon Astall, Noel Kinsey, Eddie Brown, Arthur Turner (manager), Roy Warhurst, Peter Murphy, Alex Govan. On ground: Bill Finney and Johnny Watts.

Peter 'Spud' Murphy was an excellent goalscorer, a marksman feared by defenders of all clubs. He scored 127 goals in 278 games for Blues between January 1952 and May 1961 when he retired. Formerly with Coventry City and Tottenham Hotspur, he joined Blues for £18,500 from White Hart Lane after helping Spurs win the Second Division title in 1951. He was a key figure in Blues' promotion-winning team of 1955 and appeared in the 1956 FA Cup final. Murphy died in November 1975, aged fifty-three.

Murphy scoring the all-important goal in Blues' fifth round FA Cup victory over West Bromwich Albion at a snow-covered Hawthorns in February 1956.

Back in the First Division, Blues began the 1955/56 season well, drawing two and winning two of their opening four matches. They then had a poor September before picking up again in October when they beat Spurs 3-0, Portsmouth 5-0 (away) and Manchester City 4-3. November was evenly balanced, likewise December, although the team did suffer a 6-0 drubbing at Bolton. Blues started their FA Cup campaign in January with a 7-1 win at Torquay. They won one and lost one of the two League matches played during the month and, as progress was made in the Cup, the team continued to battle on in the League where a seven-match unbeaten run shot them towards the top group. They reached the FA Cup final for the first time in twenty-five years after ousting Leyton Orient, West Bromwich Albion, Arsenal and Sunderland. But alas they fell at Wembley, losing 3-1 to Manchester City, while in the League they fought on to finish a creditable sixth. This page shows Kinsey's FA Cup final consolation goal, the programme cover (below left) and a ticket from the fixture (below right).

After their Wembley exploits in 1956, Blues were determined to go back and play under the twin towers, and they began their 1957 challenge with a third round FA Cup win over Carlisle United before slamming Southend United 6-1 at Roots Hall in round four. Here Blues' goalkeeper Gil Merrick and Roy Warhurst thwart a Shrimpers' attack. Blues progressed to the semi-finals this season after knocking out Millwall and Nottingham Forest before losing 2-0 to Manchester United at Hillsborough in front of a 65,000-plus crowd.

Inside forward Bryan Orritt scored 27 goals in 119 games for Blues between 1956 and 1962. He then moved to Middlesbrough and later went to play in Johannesburg and where he also became a prominent coach, working with black youngsters in Soweto. A Welsh under-23 international, he had the distinction (if you can call it that) of playing for Llanfairpwllgwyngyllgogerychwyrndrowl-lllantysiliogogogoch FC … and how did they get that on the transfer form?

In July 1957, after twenty-three years at St Andrew's, Birmingham-born defender Jack Badham left Blues to join non-League Stourbridge. He had given the Blues tremendous service, appearing in 190 first-class matches and scoring 4 goals. He twice helped Blues win the Second Division championship (in 1948 and 1955) and was, without reservation, a magnificent servant, occupying eight different positions but preferring a full-back berth if possible. He was unfortunate to miss the 1956 FA Cup final when Johnny Newman got the nod in preference to Jack after Roy Warhurst had been injured.

Centre half Trevor Smith played schoolboy football with and against the great Duncan Edwards and he went on to appear in 430 senior games for Blues. He joined the staff at St Andrew's as a fifteen year old in 1951, turned professional in 1953 and over the next eleven years gave Blues superb service as a dependable, rugged no-nonsense defender. He won 2 full England caps, 2 more with the 'B' team and 15 for the under-23s. He also represented his country at both schoolboy and youth team levels and twice played for the Football League XI. After leaving Blues in 1964 he joined Walsall and in later life worked as a manager for Thresher's wine store.

One of the stars of the Blues team during the fifties was wing-half Roy Warhurst. Stocky, with wavy hair and a bone-crunching tackle, he made 239 appearances for the club between 1950 and 1957. A Yorkshireman born in 1926, he joined Blues from his home town club Sheffield United and left for Manchester City. He also served with Crewe Alexandra and Oldham Athletic and later became a scrap metal dealer in Birmingham. He amassed close on 400 senior appearances during a fine career but sadly missed the match he most wanted to take part in, the 1956 FA Cup final. Injury prevented him from doing so and later he joined the team he would have played against.

Left: Former Blues Chairman Harry Morris was in office when Blues won the Second Division championship in 1954/55 and reached the FA Cup final the following season. *Right:* South African-born centre forward Ted Purdon scored 30 goals in 70 League and Cup games for Blues over a period of four years from 1950 to 1954. He then left St Andrew's for Sunderland.

A mid-1950s team group. From left to right, back row: Ken Green, Brian Farmer, Dick Neal, Johnny Schofield, Ken Fish (trainer), Trevor Smith, Gil Merrick, 'Bud' Houghton, George Allen, Johnny Watts. Middle row: Arthur Turner (joint-manager), Harry Hooper, Eddie Brown, Bryan Orritt, Peter Murphy, Jeff Hall, Gordon Astall, Billy Hume, Pat Beasley (joint-manager). Front row: Graham Sissons, David Jones, Bunny Larkin, Alex Jackson, Jimmy McLaughlin, Brian Taylor.

Former Manchester United junior Billy Rudd never really established himself at St Andrew's. He scored 4 goals in 26 senior appearances for Blues between 1959 and 1961, but during his career he amassed a fine record as an inside forward. An ex-cabinetmaker, he played in almost 650 games at club level (574 in the Football League alone), while also serving with New York All Stars, York City, Grimsby Town, Rochdale and Bury. His uncle Joe played for Manchester City.

Dick Neal was a sturdy left-half who was strong in the tackle. He played 197 games for Blues, scoring 18 goals, between April 1957 and October 1961. Sold by Wolverhampton Wanderers to Lincoln City as a twenty-one year old, he switched to St Andrew's in a deal involving Albert Linnecor. He went on to win 4 England under-23 caps and on leaving St Andrew's he joined Middlesbrough, later returning to Sincil Bank in 1963. He was replaced by Terry Hennessey in the Blues team.

Ken Green retired as a Blues player in 1959 but during the mid-fifties he was regarded as one of the best full-backs in the country. A Londoner from West Ham, he was nineteen and a half when he joined the staff at St Andrew's during the 1943/44 wartime season. He went on to play in more than 440 games for Blues and gained two England 'B' caps. He helped win promotion in 1948 and 1955 and was an FA Cup finalist with Blues in 1956. He actually signed for Blues in the dressing room of arch-rivals Aston Villa. Ken looked after a post office in Handsworth, Birmingham, during the 1970s.

Action from the First Division game against Arsenal at Highbury in April 1956. Gil Merrick saves from Gunners' left-winger Joe Haverty. Arsenal won 1-0 with Jimmy Bloomfield, who was later to sign for Blues, setting up the winning goal for Derek Tapscott.

Trevor Smith, the Blues skipper, shakes hands with his counterpart Juan Segarra of Barcelona prior to kick-off of the Inter Cities Fairs Cup semi-final second leg encounter in Spain on 13 November 1957. A crowd of 60,000 saw Blues beaten 1-0, bringing the aggregate score to 4-4. Alas, a replay in Basle went Barcelona's way by 2-1.

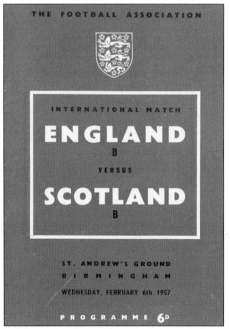

Over a period of five years, two representative matches involving England were staged at St Andrew's – a 'B' international against Scotland in February 1957 and an under 23 encounter against Greece in November 1962. In both of these matches many top class players were on view, most of them going on to win full honours for their country. The 'B' international in 1957 resulted in a 4-1 win for England while the under 23 match saw the Greeks hammered 5-0. Bobby Tambling of Chelsea scored a hat-trick and Terry Venables wore the no. 4 shirt.

When Blues played in the Inter Cities Fairs Cup for the second time (1958-60) their manager was Pat Beasley. Here, the boss (second from the right) sits in the dugout during the away game with Union St Gilloise of Luxembourg. The reserves in the picture are goalkeeper Colin Withers, striker Robin Stubbs and defender George Allen. Coach Dave Fairhurst is sitting on the extreme left.

On 30 April 1960 Blues met FA Cup finalists Blackburn Rovers in their last League game of the season. A crowd of almost 24,500 saw the contest, which resulted in a 1-0 win for Blues, Johnny Gordon scoring the all-important goal. Here, Peter Murphy (extreme right) chases a through ball into the Rovers penalty area.

Robin Stubbs scores the first of his two goals in Blues' 2-0 home win over Arsenal in a Division One match at St Andrew's in September 1960. Tommy Docherty, later to manage Manchester United and Wolves, is the player attempting to stop Stubbs clipping the ball over goalkeeper Jack Kelsey. Stubbs netted 20 goals in 70 games for Blues between 1958 and 1963 before moving to Torquay.

For three years Blues were well served by right-winger Harry Hooper who joined them from Wolverhampton Wanderers for £25,000 in 1957. Having started his League career in London with West Ham United, he scored 42 goals in 119 outings for Blues and also made several of Robin Stubbs' goals as well. On leaving St Andrew's Hooper signed for Sunderland. He won six England 'B' caps, played twice for the under 23s and also represented the Football League. His father Harry senior played for Sheffield United and his brother Alf for Halifax Town.

In April 1961 Blues visited Italy to play Inter Milan in the first leg of the Inter Cities Fairs Cup semi-final. This photograph shows Blues' centre forward Jimmy Harris scoring his side's first goal in their excellent 2-1 victory in front of 20,000 fans in the San Siro stadium. Blues also won the return leg by the same score and went through to the final 4-2 on aggregate. Unfortunately, they could not beat another Italian team, AS Roma, and went down 4-2 on aggregate to lose their second Fairs Cup final in successive seasons. They had lost the 1960 showdown with Barcelona 4-1 on aggregate. *Right:* The programme for the home leg against Inter Milan.

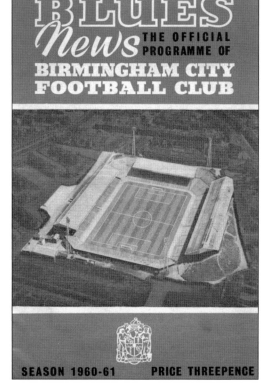

BLUES
news THE OFFICIAL PROGRAMME OF
BIRMINGHAM CITY FOOTBALL CLUB

SEASON 1960-61   PRICE THREEPENCE

En route to the 1961 Inter Cities Fairs Cup final Blues defeated the Hungarian side Ujpesti Dozsa 5-3 on aggregate in the opening round. After a 3-2 home victory Blues travelled to Budapest and won 2-1, thus becoming the first British club side to win in Hungary for twenty-five years. Here, the players line up before the start of the return leg in Budapest. Johnny Gordon (far left) scored twice in the win at St Andrew's.

Johnny Gordon was an all-action inside forward who scored a goal every four games during a fine League career which spanned eighteen years from 1949 to 1967. He joined Blues from Portsmouth for £10,000 in 1958 and returned to Fratton Park in March 1961. The following season he helped Pompey win the Third Division championship. Gordon scored 40 goals in 115 games for Blues and 105 in 443 League outings all told.

Between them these eleven players accumulated almost 2,250 senior appearances for Blues with Beard and Smith both amassing more than 400 each. From left to right, back row: Graham Sissons, Trevor Smith, Johnny Schofield, Stan Lynn, Malcolm Beard, Terry Hennessey. Front row: Mike Helliwell, Bryan Orritt, Jimmy Harris, Ken Leek, Bertie Auld.

Scotland international left-winger Bertie Auld played for his country three times and represented the Scottish League XI twice. He was a fiery character but nevertheless a marvellously gifted footballer and a real crowd-pleaser. He won medals galore with Celtic, including European Cup and World Club championships, before joining Blues in April 1961 for £15,000. He netted 31 goals in his 147 outings during his four years at St Andrew's before returning to Parkhead in 1965 for £12,000. He later assisted Hibernian and also managed Partick Thistle, Dumbarton, Hibernian and Hamilton Academical.

Action from Blues' 3-2 home League win over rivals Aston Villa in October 1962. *Above:* Stan 'The Wham' Lynn hammers in a penalty against his former club for Blues' first equalizer. *Below:* Ken Leek heads in Blues' second goal to make it 2-2. A crowd of 42,207 saw Leek grab the winner late in the second half.

Six
League Cup Joy,
Relegation and Francis

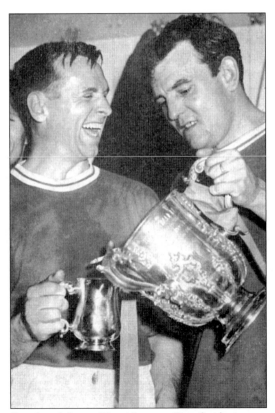

Stan Lynn and Trevor Smith celebrate Blues' League Cup final victory over rivals Aston Villa in 1963. The first leg ended 0-0 at Villa Park before Blues won the return clash at St Andrew's by 3-1 to win their first ever major League or Cup competition.

A goal for Bertie Auld in Blues' 3-3 home draw with Nottingham Forest in November 1963. Later in the season Forest whipped Blues 4-0 at The City Ground.

In December 1963 Blues entertained Fulham in a First Division match at St Andrew's. In this picture two Cottagers' players, Johnny Key and Bobby Robson, lunge forward in an attempt to rob Jimmy Bloomfield of possession. The game ended goal-less.

Blues' goalkeeper Johnny Schofield palms away a right-wing centre during the home League game with Blackpool in April 1963. The rampant Seasiders went to town and won 6-3 in front of just over 15,000 hardy supporters.

Welsh international left-back Colin Green made his debut for Blues in December 1962 in a 2-0 home defeat against Tottenham Hotspur. He took over from Graham Sissons and went on to make 217 senior appearances for the club before quitting League action in 1971. Green was capped 15 times by his country.

The Birmingham City team from 1963. From left to right, back row: Malcolm Beard, Stan Lynn, Colin Withers, Winston Foster, Terry Hennessey, Colin Green. Front row: Mike Helliwell, Ken Leek, Jimmy Bloomfield (with mascot), Peter Bullock, Bertie Auld.

Welsh international inside forward Ken Leek was born deep in Rugby Union territory near Pontypridd. However, instead of passing the oval ball around he became a star performer with the round one. During a fine soccer career he scored almost 150 goals in 397 League appearances while serving Northampton Town, Leicester City, Newcastle United, Blues (from November 1961 to December 1964), Northampton Town (again) and Bradford City. He was capped 13 times by Wales and helped Blues win the League Cup in 1963.

Mike Helliwell (not in picture) has a shot deflected past the post by the legs of Wolves' goalkeeper Fred Davies during the Midlands derby at St Andrew's in October 1963. The outcome of a close encounter was a 2-2 draw. Alex Harley and Dave Woodfield (own goal) scored for Blues while wingers Alan Hinton and Terry Wharton replied for Wolves. The attendance was 24,804.

Voted Midlands Footballer of the Year in 1963, Welsh international wing-half Terry Hennessey was a creative, intelligent player with superb vision, great passing ability and composure. He joined Blues as a youngster, turned professional in 1959 and went on to appear in more than 200 games for the club before leaving to sign for Nottingham Forest in 1965. He later played for Derby County. Capped 39 times by Wales, he also collected 6 at under-23 level and played for Blues in the 1961 Fairs Cup final and 1963 League Cup final and later won a First Division championship medal with Derby.

A young Trevor Francis is denied a scoring opportunity by Watford 'keeper Derek Edmonds during a Second Division game at St Andrew's in March 1971. Blues eventually won 2-0 with Francis on target. The Plymouth-born inside forward went on to claim 133 goals in 329 games for Blues before becoming Britain's first £1 million footballer when he joined Nottingham Forest in 1979. Thereafter he assisted several English clubs, gained 52 full caps and played in America, Scotland and Italy. After retiring he became a manager with QPR and Sheffield Wednesday, and then in May 1996 he returned to St Andrew's to take charge of Blues. Francis scored four goals against Bolton in 1970 when he was just sixteen years of age.

In 1967/68 Blues reached the semi-final of the FA Cup. They failed to make it to Wembley, losing 2-0 to neighbours West Bromwich Albion at neutral Villa Park, despite a gritty performance. *Above:* the Blues squad for that season: From left to right, back row: Garry Pendrey, Colin Green, Dennis Thwaites, Malcolm Page. Middle row: Geoff Vowden, Malcolm Beard, Phil Summerill, Jim Herriot, John Sharples, John Slueenwenhoek, Micky Darrell. Front row: Winston Foster, Trevor Hockey, Ray Martin, Ron Wylie (captain), Fred Pickering, Bert Murray, Johnny Vincent. In the third round of the competition Blues ousted Halifax Town 4-2 at The Shay. They then accounted for Leyton Orient 3-0 at home and in round five Barry Bridges scored two goals to give Blues a 2-1 home win over Arsenal after the sides had drawn 1-1 at Highbury. A Fred Pickering goal at St Andrew's took Blues into the semi-final at Chelsea's expense. *Below:* a packed St Andrew's watches Chelsea 'keeper Peter Bonetti gather a right wing cross with Barry Bridges (white shirt) the Blues striker waiting for a slip.

Manager Stan Cullis was appointed to the hot seat at St Andrew's in December 1965 and he remained in office until March 1970. Born in Ellesmere Port, Cheshire, in 1915, as a player Cullis was a dominant centre half who gave Wolves and England great service before and during the war. He retired as a player in 1948 to become manager at Molineux and he duly guided Wolves to three League championships, two FA Cup final victories and into Europe. As boss of Blues he saw his team reach the 1967 League Cup semi-final and the 1968 FA Cup semi-final but he failed to win promotion. Blues' best effort was to finish fourth in Division Two in 1968. Cullis is now resident in Malvern.

Fred Pickering was once a full-back but developed into an exceptionally fine centre forward: a goalscorer, a target man and a player who gave as good as he got out on the field. He played 88 times for Blues and scored 32 goals during his two seasons at St Andrew's. He joined Blues from Everton for £50,000 in August 1967 and left for Blackpool in June 1969. Prior to his service at Goodison Park, Pickering had been with Blackburn Rovers and after leaving Bloomfield Road he returned to Ewood Park for a second spell in 1971. Capped three times by England at senior level, Pickering scored a hat-trick on his international debut in a 10-0 win over the USA. He also represented his country's under 23 team and played for the Football League.

The cover and centre spread of the matchday programme printed for the Blues versus Aston Villa Second Division game at St Andrew's in February 1968. Over 45,000 fans saw Blues win 2-1, both goals coming from former Chelsea utility forward Barry Bridges. This was Blues' first League double over their arch-rivals for ten years. Earlier in the season Blues had won 4-2 at Villa Park when Bridges also scored twice in front of almost 50,000 spectators. Of the 96 encounters between the two clubs in the Football League, Blues have only 32 against Villa's tally of 39. Almost 300 goals have been scored, 144 by Blues. The last time the teams played each other at League level was in season 1987/88 – let's hope the next time is in the Premiership!

BIRMINGHAM CITY F.C.

ASTON VILLA
24th FEBRUARY 1968
OFFICIAL 1/-

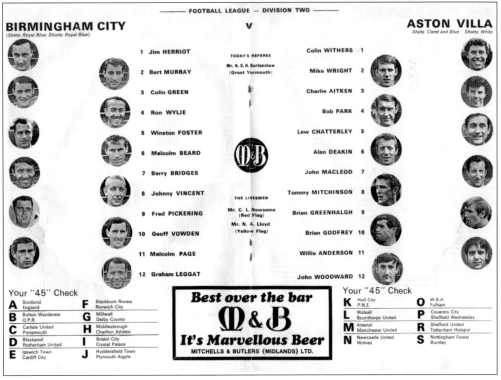

———— FOOTBALL LEAGUE — DIVISION TWO ————

BIRMINGHAM CITY
(Shirts: Royal Blue; Shorts: Royal Blue).

ASTON VILLA
Shirts: Claret and Blue   Shorts: White

BIRMINGHAM CITY		ASTON VILLA
1 Jim HERRIOT	TODAY'S REFEREE Mr. N. C. H. Burtenshaw (Great Yarmouth)	Colin WITHERS 1
2 Bert MURRAY		Mike WRIGHT 2
3 Colin GREEN		Charlie AITKEN 3
4 Ron WYLIE		Bob PARK 4
5 Winston FOSTER		Lew CHATTERLEY 5
6 Malcolm BEARD	M&B	Alan DEAKIN 6
7 Barry BRIDGES		John MACLEOD 7
8 Johnny VINCENT	THE LINESMEN	Tommy MITCHINSON 8
9 Fred PICKERING	Mr. C. L. Newsome (Red Flag)	Brian GREENHALGH 9
10 Geoff VOWDEN	Mr. N. A. Lloyd (Yellow Flag)	Brian GODFREY 10
11 Malcolm PAGE		Willie ANDERSON 11
12 Graham LEGGAT		John WOODWARD 12

Your "45" Check

A	Scotland England	F	Blackburn Rovers Norwich City
B	Bolton Wanderers Q.P.R.	G	Millwall Derby County
C	Carlisle United Portsmouth	H	Middlesbrough Charlton Athletic
D	Blackpool Rotherham United	I	Bristol City Crystal Palace
E	Ipswich Town Cardiff City	J	Huddersfield Town Plymouth Argyle

Your "45" Check

K	Hull City P.N.E.	O	W.B.A. Fulham
L	Walsall Scunthorpe United	P	Coventry City Sheffield Wednesday
M	Arsenal Manchester United	R	Sheffield United Tottenham Hotspur
N	Newcastle United Wolves	S	Nottingham Forest Burnley

In October 1968 a nine-goal thriller at St Andrew's saw Blues defeat Fulham 5-4. The hero of the hour was Blues striker Jimmy Greenhoff who scored four times, including this terrific header. Greenhoff had a fine career, mainly serving Leeds United, Manchester United and Stoke City. His record with Blues between 1968 and 1969 was 15 goals in just 36 appearances.

Dennis Thwaites had a sweet left foot and here he is scoring for Blues against Sheffield Wednesday at Hillsborough in a fourth round FA Cup-tie in January 1969. A crowd of over 52,000 saw Blues earn a 2-2 draw, but then at St Andrew's they failed to capitalize on home advantage and lost the replay 2-1. Thwaites was a direct left-winger who netted 21 goals in almost 100 first team games for Blues whom he served as a professional for ten years from 1962 to 1972.

Welsh international midfielder Trevor Hockey was a nomadic footballer who served with twelve different clubs during an eventful career which spanned almost eighteen years. Born in Yorkshire in 1943, he played rugby as a youngster but then turned to soccer and signed professional forms with Bradford City in 1960. Thereafter he did the rounds, playing in turn for Nottingham Forest, Newcastle United, Blues (from November 1965 to January 1971), Sheffield United, Norwich City, Aston Villa, Bradford City (again), Athlone Town as player-manager, San Diego Jaws, San José Earthquakes and Los Angeles Quicksilver (on three separate visits to the NASL) and Stalybridge Celtic as player-coach-manager. Hockey won 9 full caps for Wales and was one of the first players to play for that country via parentage qualification. For Blues he scored 13 goals in 232 appearances. While a player he turned out on all 92 League grounds during the 1960s and he also went on stage to do a concert. A real joker at times, Hockey sadly died of a heart attack in his home town of Keighley in April 1967, shortly after playing in a five-a-side game.

Between them the two Malcolms – Beard (left) and Page (right) – amassed more than 800 appearances for Blues. Both players occupied similar positions in defence and midfield and were terrific club men, always giving 110 per cent out of the field. Beard was born in Cannock in 1942 and joined Blues as a youngster before turning professional in 1959. He remained at St Andrew's until 1971 when he moved to neighbouring Villa Park. He starred in 405 first team games for the club, scoring 32 goals, and won a League Cup tankard in 1963 and a Fairs Cup runners-up medal in 1961. Page was born in mid-Wales in 1947 and he became a professional at St Andrew's in 1964. He stayed at St Andrew's for 17 seasons and played in 394 games for Blues, scoring 10 goals and helping the team gain promotion to the First Division in 1972. He also represented Wales 28 times – thus becoming Blues' most-capped player – and he also bagged a handful of schoolboy caps as well as six at under 23 level. He left St Andrew's in 1981 to sign for Oxford United.

In 1972 Blues entered the Anglo-Italian Cup competition. They played four games, beating Lanerossi Vicenza 5-3 and Sampdoria 2-0 at home, but lost to the latter 2-1 and drew with Vicenza 0-0 in Italy, thus failing to make progress from their group.

Seven
Back in the First and Ramsey as Manager

Howard Kendall joined Blues from Everton in 1974 in a deal which took Bob Latchford to Goodison Park. Here, Blues fanatic and top comedian Jasper Carrott gives the thumbs up to manager Freddie Goodwin on the signing.

Another goal for Bob Latchford, this one coming in Blues' 3-1 victory over Ipswich Town at Portman Road in the League Cup in November 1973. Blues were ousted by Plymouth Argyle at the next stage of the competition having beaten Blackpool and Newcastle United in the opening two rounds.

Latchford scored 84 goals in 194 first team games for Blues before moving to Everton in a player-exchange deal involving Howard Kendall. He went on to win a total of 12 full England caps and 6 at under 23 level. In 1982 and 1983, as a player with Merthyr Tydfil, he collected two Welsh Cup winners medals. Latchford, who later returned to join the backroom staff at St Andrew's, scored 138 goals in 288 games during his seven years at Goodison Park.

These two players were often mistaken for each other – and you can see why. On the left is Tony Towers, who also played for Manchester City and Sunderland as well as Vancouver Whitecaps, Tampa Bay Rowdies and Montreal Manic, and on the right is defender Pat Howard who assisted Barnsley, Newcastle United, Arsenal, Portland Timbers and Bury. Both were together at St Andrew's in 1977/78 with Towers staying with Blues until 1981.

Over a period of six years from 1970 to 1976 Alan Campbell gave Blues tremendous service in the centre of the field. The influential long-haired Scotsman from Arbroath appeared in 210 games and scored 14 goals, helping Blues win the Second Division title in 1972. He started his senior career with Charlton Athletic and joined Blues from Cardiff City. He left St Andrew's for Carlisle United and dropped out of League football in 1982. He played once for the Scottish under 23 team.

Archie Gemmill leads out Blues for a live TV match. It must have been a great moment for the little boy mascot.

Texaco Cup semi-final programme. In this 1974 semi-final encounter Blues succumbed 4-2 on aggregate to the Magpies in this short-lived sponsored competition. The first leg ended 1-1 at St Andrew's but the initial second leg at St James' Park was abandoned because of bad light after 100 minutes with the scores again level at 1-1. The replay went United's way 3-1 and Blues were out. In their first tie Blues defeated Stoke City 3-1 on penalties after the two-legged tussle had finished goal-less.

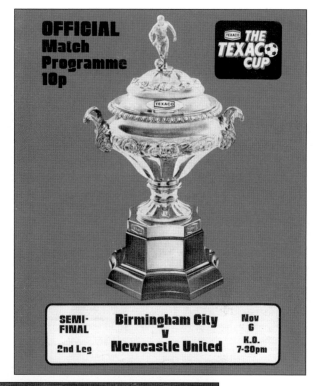

The programme for the 1975 FA Cup semi-final against Fulham. Blues lost to the Cottagers 1-0 in a replay at Maine Road after the Hillsborough semi-final had finished level at 1-1.

Above left: Stan Harland, an ex-Swindon Town player who had helped the Robins win the League Cup, Anglo-Italian Cup and the Third Division title. He made 50 appearances for Blues. *Above right:* Joe Gallagher, a Liverpudlian who made 335 appearances for Blues before moving to Wolverhampton Wanderers. A solid performer, he also assisted Burnley and was capped for England at 'B' team level. *Below right:* Phil Summerill in action for Blues against Charlton Athletic in 1969/70. He was a very useful goalscorer who netted 52 times in 131 outings for Blues between 1964 and 1973. Born in Villa territory (Erdington) in 1947, he helped Blues win promotion in 1972 before joining Huddersfield Town and later Millwall and Wimbledon. *Below left:* Geoff Vowden played in the same forward line as Summerill in the late 1960s. He was a fine goalscorer who found the net over 150 times for his three major clubs: Nottingham Forest, Blues and Aston Villa. He played at St Andrew's from October 1964 to March 1971, during which time he notched 94 goals in 253 first team outings for Blues.

Inside forward Bobby Hope played well over 400 games for West Bromwich Albion and won two full caps for Scotland before he joined Blues for the unusual fee of £66,666 in May 1972. He went on to appear in 48 games during his short stay at St Andrew's which ended in April 1975 when he chose to try his luck in the NASL. Hope later played for Sheffield Wednesday during the 1976/77 season, did some scouting for Wolverhampton Wanderers and managed non-League Bromsgrove Rovers before returning to The Hawthorns as youth development officer, a position he holds today.

On 21 November 1974 two popular pubs in the Bull Ring area of Birmingham were bombed by the IRA. A total of 19 people were killed and over 100 injured. On the evening of Monday 9 December, as part of the fundraising scheme organised by the Lord Mayor of Birmingham, Cllr E. James Eames, a challenge match featuring a West Midlands XI against an All Star XI was staged at Blues' St Andrew's ground. Several big name players participated in the match including Peter Shilton and Alan Hudson (both from Stoke City), Gerry Francis (QPR), John Richards (Wolves) and the Birmingham City trio of Kenny Burns, Howard Kendall and goalkeeper Dave Latchford.

WEST MIDLANDS XI v ALL STARS XI

ST. ANDREW'S, BIRMINGHAM, MONDAY, DECEMBER 9th, 1974, k.o. 7.30 p.m. Official Souvenir Prog. 10p

Blues players acknowledge their supporters prior to their penultimate League game of the 1971/72 season away at Sheffield Wednesday. Skipper Alan Campbell (extreme right) is joined in the centre circle by George Smith, Malcolm Page, Bob Hatton, Bob Latchford, Roger Hynd, Gordon Taylor, goalkeeper Paul Cooper, Garry Pendrey and Alan Whitehead. Blues won the game 2-1 and three days later beat Leyton Orient 1-0 in London to clinch promotion to the First Division.

Left-winger Gordon Taylor made his senior debut for Bolton Wanderers in 1962. He moved from Burnden Park to St Andrew's in 1969 and scored 10 goals in 203 games for Blues, helping them win promotion in 1972 before transferring to Blackburn Rovers in 1976. He also played for Vancouver Whitecaps and Bury before retiring to join the PFA. Taylor also possesses a BSc in Economics and during a fine career he amassed over 700 League and Cup appearances in England alone.

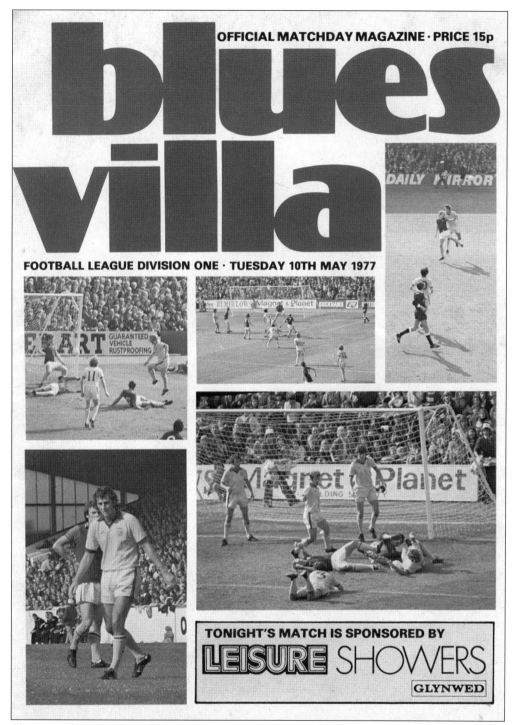

OFFICIAL MATCHDAY MAGAZINE · PRICE 15p

blues villa

FOOTBALL LEAGUE DIVISION ONE · TUESDAY 10TH MAY 1977

DAILY MIRROR

GUARANTEED VEHICLE RUSTPROOFING

TONIGHT'S MATCH IS SPONSORED BY

LEISURE SHOWERS

GLYNWED

Blues' match versus Aston Villa in May 1977. Earlier in the season – on 18 September 1976 – a crowd of more than 50,000 had seen Blues beat their arch-rivals Aston Villa 2-1 at Villa Park. For the return encounter 43,721 assembled at St Andrew's and again the result favoured Blues who gained another 2-1 victory.

Scottish international Kenny Burns was just as effective in attack as he was in defence and scored 53 goals in 204 outings for Blues between 1971 and 1977. A Glaswegian born in 1953, he left St Andrew's in a £150,000 deal with Nottingham Forest in 1977 and four years later he switched to Leeds United, having helped Brian Clough's men win the European Cup twice, take the First Division championship and also the League Cup. After Leeds he assisted Derby County, Notts County and Barnsley and also played in Sweden for Elfsborg. Burns, who was as tough as they come, was voted Footballer of the Year in 1978 and won a total of 20 caps for his country.

Jim Smith is still in football today, forty-five years after having a trial as a schoolboy for Sheffield United. He went on to play for the Blades as well as Aldershot, Halifax Town, Lincoln City, Boston United and Colchester United, managing the latter two clubs. He then took charge of Blues from March 1978 to February 1982, replacing England's World Cup winning supremo Sir Alf Ramsey in the hot seat at St Andrew's. On leaving Blues, Smith took over at Oxford United and then in turn he managed QPR, Newcastle United and Portsmouth before guiding Derby County into the Premiership. Under his leadership Blues won promotion from the Second Division in 1980.

Frank Worthington joined Blues in 1979 and was a great asset to the team which won promotion the following year. The flamboyant centre forward and avid Elvis Presley fanatic scored 33 goals in 88 games for Blues before leaving St Andrew's to join Leeds United in 1982. His career in football spanned almost thirty years from 1964 to 1992 inclusive. Capped eight times by England, he also served with Huddersfield Town, Bolton, Leicester City and Philadelphia Fury among others.

Blues goalkeeper Dave Latchford had a testimonial match before he left St Andrew's and this picture shows him surrounded by some great players: Bob Hatton (extreme left), George Smith, the late Terry Hibbitt, Pat Howard, Barry Bridges (with beard), Gordon Taylor, Bob Latchford, the moustached Garry Pendrey, winger John Connolly, Joe Gallagher, Jimmy Calderwood and Keith Bertschin (extreme right). Latchford made 239 appearances between the posts for Blues for whom he signed as a professional in 1966, remaining at St Andrew's until 1977 when he moved to Motherwell.

Defender Garry Pendrey appeared in 360 League and Cup matches for Blues over a period of thirteen years from 1966 to 1979. He developed through the club's junior ranks and skippered the youngsters in 1967 when they reached the FA Youth Cup final. He was a key member of the Blues side that won promotion in 1972. The club he joined on leaving St Andrew's, West Bromwich Albion, were Blues' opponents in his testimonial match. Pendrey, who also played for Torquay United, Bristol Rovers and Walsall, later managed Blues from 1987 until 1989, coached at Wolves and is now on the coaching staff at Premiership club Coventry City.

In 1978 Blues signed Alan Buckley from Walsall to boost their strike-force. The twenty-seven year old had started his career with Nottingham Forest before joining the Saddlers. He did well enough with Blues, scoring 8 goals in 29 games, including this one against Manchester United at St Andrew's in November 1978 when Blues triumphed 5-1. He returned to Fellows Park at the end of the 1978/79 season and went on to score well over 200 goals for Walsall, later managing the club. He then guided Grimsby Town to promotion from the Fourth to the Second Division in double quick time before having a spell in charge at West Bromwich Albion. He returned as boss of the Mariners in May 1997.

Republic of Ireland international Don Givens scores for Blues against Coventry City at Highfield Road in a First Division game in October 1978. His effort, however, was all to no avail as the Sky Blues won 2-1. Givens, capped 56 times by the Republic of Ireland, scored 19 goals for his country but only 10 for Blues in 64 appearances for the club between 1978 and 1981. During his career the Dublin-born forward also played and scored for Manchester United, Luton, QPR, Bournemouth, Sheffield United and Xamac Neuchatel in Switzerland.

In September 1978 Blues boss Jim Smith signed the Argentinian World Cup-winning defender Alberto Tarantini from Boca Juniors for £250,000. Tarantini is second from the left between Malcolm Page and Tony Towers with Don Givens on the extreme right. He made just 24 appearances for Blues before leaving the club for Tallares Cordoba in May 1979. He was capped 59 times by his country.

The playing career of goalkeeper Roger Jones spanned almost twenty-five years. He entered professional football with Portsmouth in the early 1960s and retired in 1985 with over 750 League appearances under his belt. He served on loan with Blues in February and March 1982, having just four outings between the posts. Among the other clubs he represented were Bournemouth, Blackburn Rovers, Newcastle United, Stoke City, Derby County and York City. He gained League Division Three and Four honours with Blackburn and York respectively.

Nicky Platnauer, pictured during a training spell, made just 36 appearances for Blues between December 1984 and September 1986. In a useful career, however, the versatile and nomadic Leicester-born player had close on 500 games in various competitions while also serving with Bristol Rovers, Coventry City, Reading, Cardiff City, Notts County, Port Vale, Leicester City, Scunthorpe United, Mansfield Town and Lincoln City. He was a bank clerk before entering the world of soccer.

Kevan Broadhurst made 173 appearances for Blues as a defender and midfielder, scoring 10 goals. Unfortunately, injury forced the Dewsbury-born utility player into an early retirement in 1986 after eight good seasons at St Andrew's. He also had a spell on loan with nearby Walsall in 1979.

Midfielder Ian Handysides' life ended tragically in August 1990 when he died of a brain tumour. He was only twenty-seven and had played 133 games for Blues in two spells at the club. He first signed as a professional at St Andrew's in January 1980 and returned there from Walsall for £17,000 in January 1984. Capped by England at youth team level, he helped Blues win promotion from Division Two before leaving to try his luck with the Saddlers.

Julian Dicks, pictured here with Lee Dixon (then of Stoke City), was a tough-tackling full-back and a determined competitor who always enjoyed a challenge. Dicks made 102 appearances for Blues before transferring to West Ham United for £400,000 in March 1988. He then had a spell with Liverpool only to return to Upton Park in November 1994. Capped four times by England at under-21 level, he passed the career milestone of 500 club appearances with the Hammers in 1999.

Ian Handysides scoring one of his 27 goals for Blues in the local Second City derby against rivals Aston Villa at St Andrew's in December 1982. Blues won the game 3-0 in front of 43,864 spectators.

Blues signed full-back 'Harry' Roberts from Coventry City for £10,000, with the cash obtained as a result of the Buy a Player Fund organized by supporters. Born in Manchester in 1955, Roberts made over 200 appearances during his time at Highfield Road, which ended when he moved to St Andrew's in March 1984. He made a further 213 appearances for Blues and later played for Wolves from 1990 to 1992. He had to work overtime to see off the boo-boys at St Andrew's.

In May 1983 a crowd of just under 15,000 saw Blues held to a 1-1 draw at St Andrew's by Brighton and Hove Albion who were soon to play in the FA Cup final against Manchester United. This photograph shows Blues' centre forward Mick Ferguson getting between defenders Steve Walford and Steve Foster to head goalwards. Ian Handysides netted for Blues in this game.

Eight
New Managers and a Deserted Stadium

Tony Towers (Blues) and Leicester City's Dennis Rofe go through the formalities before a League game at St Andrew's.

Ron Saunders was the Blues manager who re-signed Handysides. The former Everton, Portsmouth, Gillingham, Watford and Charlton Athletic centre forward, who scored over 200 goals in more than 400 League games between 1951 and 1967, was forty-nine years of age when he took over from Jim Smith in the hot seat at St Andrew's in February 1982. He had previously managed Oxford United, Manchester City, Norwich City and Blues' arch-rivals Aston Villa. He remained in charge at Blues until January 1986 when he moved across to take over at another Midlands club, West Bromwich Albion. Saunders took Norwich, Manchester City and Villa to Wembley and guided the latter to the Football League championship in 1981.

The former Tottenham Hotspur and Derby County wing-half Dave Mackay (pictured here with the Kumar brothers who bought the club for £1.6 million in 1989) served as Blues' manager from April 1989 to January 1991. The Scottish international from Edinburgh also managed Swindon Town, Nottingham Forest, his former club Derby, Walsall and Doncaster Rovers. In his playing days Mackay amassed in excess of 600 appearances as a professional and he also gained 22 caps for his country. In 1969 he was voted the Football Writers' Player of the Year.

Following promotion from Division Two, Blues revisited Midlands rivals West Bromwich Albion in the top flight in October 1985, but sadly they lost the local derby by two goals to one in front of 14,576 spectators. Here, Blues defenders Ken Armstrong and Nicky Platnauer are challenged by Albion's Martyn Bennett.

John Bond, the former West Ham United defender and Norwich City and Manchester City boss, was in charge of Blues for a little over fifteen months from January 1986 to May 1987. Unfortunately, he failed to bring success to St Andrew's and was dismissed shortly after Blues had avoided relegation to the Third Division. Bond was still in football in 1999/2000 with Carlisle United.

Colin Brazier (top left), Phil Hawker (top right) and Kevin Summerfield (bottom left) were all associated with both Blues and Walsall during their respective careers. Brazier also played for Wolves and Kidderminster Harriers; Hawker had one game on loan with West Bromwich Albion, while Summerfield also served with the Baggies as well as Plymouth Argyle, Cardiff City, Exeter and Shrewsbury Town. Between them the trio amassed more than 1,000 appearances as professionals.

Defender Graham Forbes of Walsall battles with Blues' Dean Peer during the League game at Fellows Park in March 1990. Blues got the better of the Saddlers by a goal to nil in this Third Division fixture, Nigel Gleghorn scoring the all-important winner in front of just 6,036 fans.

On 29 February 1992, sixth-placed Blues met top-of-the-table Stoke City in a vital Second Division promotion game at St Andrew's. Over 22,000 spectators witnessed the first 89 minutes of the 1-1 draw, but there were barely 20 people inside the ground to see the remaining 3 minutes. John Frain had given Blues the lead from the penalty spot midway through the first half but with time running out Stoke equalized with a hotly disputed goal by Paul Barnes (who was later to play and score for Blues). This caused irate fans to riot on the pitch. The referee, Roger Wiseman, immediately took the players off and said that he would not restart the game until the ground was emptied. This was done, the players reappeared and they duly played out the last minute plus added time at walking pace.

Terry Cooper was manager of Bristol City and Exeter City prior to moving in at St Andrew's. He held the post for two years and four months guiding Blues to promotion from Division Three in his first full season in charge (1991/92). Under his control Blues played 112 games and were undefeated in 70 of them.

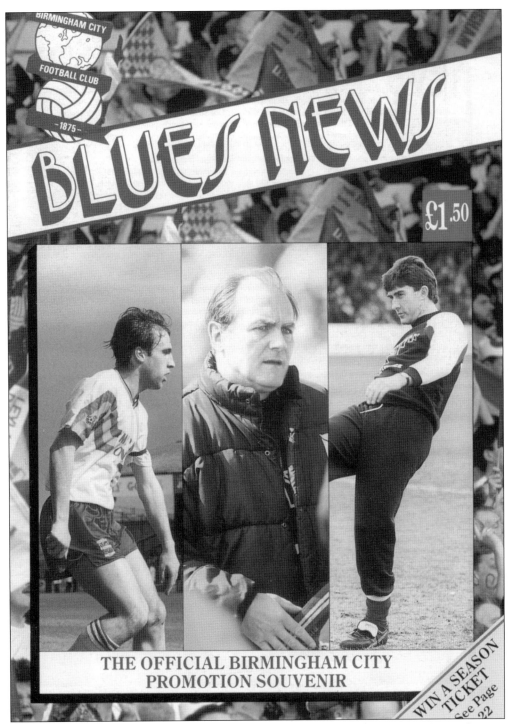

THE OFFICIAL BIRMINGHAM CITY
PROMOTION SOUVENIR

£1.50

WIN A SEASON TICKET See Page 22

The Blues promotion booklet from the 1991/92 season when, under manager Terry Cooper, Blues won promotion from the Third Division by finishing runners-up in the table with 81 points, one behind the champions Brentford. Blues lost only two home matches, scored a total of 69 goals, conceded 52 and the average League attendance at St Andrew's was 12,433.

Veteran goalkeeper Mark Prudhoe (left) and rugged defender Vince Overson (right) played for both Blues and Stoke City during their respective footballing careers. Prudhoe was a soccer nomad who served with more than a dozen League clubs during a fine career which spanned seventeen years from 1981 to 1998. Overson, too, has had an excellent career which has also seen him play for Burnley and Shrewsbury Town. Prudhoe, signed from Sunderland in 1984 and transferred to Walsall in 1986, made just 5 senior appearances for Blues while Overson, who was recruited from Turf Moor in 1986 and sold to Stoke City five years later, scored 5 goals in his 209 League and Cup outings for Blues.

Midfielder Nigel Gleghorn (left) and striker Paul Peschisolido (right) are two more players who have been associated with both Blues and Stoke City. Gleghorn played for Ipswich Town and Manchester City before joining Blues for £175,000 in 1989. He went from St Andrew's to Stoke City for £100,000 in 1992 and later assisted Burnley, Brentford and Northampton Town before entering non-League soccer in 1999. Gleghorn's record with Blues was 42 goals in 176 appearances. Peschisolido had two spells with Blues. The Canadian international, capped almost 40 times by his country, was at St Andrew's from 1992 to 1994 and again in 1996. He has also played for Toronto Blizzard, West Bromwich Albion and Fulham, and helped the Cottagers gain promotion to the First Division in 1999. His full record with Blues was 18 goals in 57 senior appearances.

Blues met Brentford in the two-legged Leyland DAF Cup Southern Area final in March/April 1991. A special A4 sized programme was produced by the club for the home clash with the Bees and in front of 16,129 fans Blues gained a 2-1 advantage to take to Griffin Park. In London they defeated the Bees 1-0 to go through to Wembley 3-1 on aggregate.

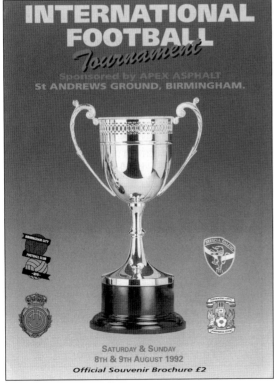

In August 1992 a four-team international tournament was staged at St Andrew's, Blues joining forces with Brescia Calcio (Italy), RCD Mallorca (Spain) and near neighbours Coventry City.

Striker Paul Moulden spent two years with Blues from 1993 until 1995. In that time he scored 6 goals in 23 outings. Earlier in his career he had been with Manchester City, Bournemouth, Oldham Athletic and Brighton, and on leaving St Andrew's he joined Huddersfield Town. Playing for the Bolton Boys' Club as a teenager, Moulden scored 289 goals in the 1981/82 season and duly got himself into the *Guinness Book of Records*. He is now with Castleton FC.

John Gayle was another useful goalscorer who found the net 14 times in 55 outings for Blues, with perhaps his best two efforts coming at Wembley in 1991 when Tranmere Rovers were defeated 3-2 in the Leyland DAF final. His first strike was a cracking twenty-five yard drive and his second a splendidly executed overhead kick. Around 40,000 Blues fans boosted the crowd that day to 58,756. He joined Blues from Wimbledon in 1990 and left St Andrew's for Coventry City in 1993.

Lou Macari was in charge of Blues when they won the Leyland Daf Trophy at Wembley in 1991. The former Scottish international, who played for Celtic and Manchester United, remained in office at St Andrew's for barely five months – from February to June 1991 – before leaving for Stoke City, taking his skipper Overson with him. He later became boss of his former club Celtic and during his career he also managed Swindon Town and had a second spell in charge of Stoke.

Paul Barnes scored 7 goals in his 15 first team outings for Blues. He joined the club from York City for £350,000 in 1992 and after four uneasy years at St Andrew's he left for Burnley, also for £350,000. He later assisted Huddersfield Town and Bury. Prior to arriving at Blues, Barnes' York tally had amounted to 85 in 179 appearances and he had also scored goals for Notts County, Stoke City and Chesterfield.

Barry Fry moved in as Blues boss in December 1993. The controversial but enthusiastic former Barnet and Southend United manager brought an air of amusement and optimism to the club and almost immediately things started to happen. He introduced player after player and in 1995 he guided Blues to the 'double': the Second Division championship and victory in the Auto Windscreen Shield at Wembley. He held office until June 1996 and then almost at once stepped back into football as manager of Peterborough United.

Experienced central defender Chris Whyte made 89 appearances for Blues following his transfer from Leeds United in 1993. Steady and reliable, the former Crystal Palace, Arsenal and West Bromwich Albion man added strength and resilience to Blues' back division before moving to Charlton Athletic in 1996.

Paul Tait scored Blues' winning goal – the first ever sudden death strike at Wembley – in the 1995 Auto Windscreen Shield final with Carlisle United. An industrious midfielder, Tait made over 200 appearances for the St Andrew's club before transferring to Oxford United in January 1999.

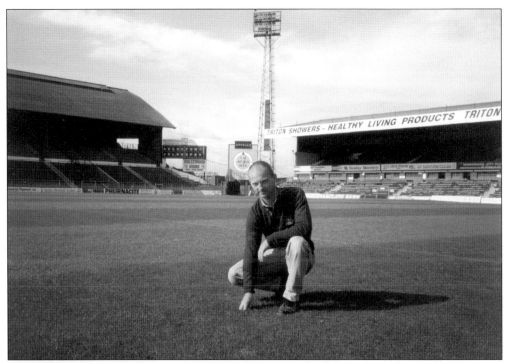

Former West Bromwich Albion groundsman Brian Harris checks the pitch at St Andrew's.

Striker Andy Saville was with Blues from March 1993 to July 1995 and during that time scored 18 goals in 65 appearances. The former Hull City, Walsall, Burnley and Hartlepool United player became a firm favourite with the St Andrew's crowd, some of whom were none too pleased when he left the club for Preston North End in a £100,000 deal. He later played for Wigan Athletic, Cardiff City and Scarborough and has also been on loan with Burnley and Hull City.

Nine
Francis' Return and Premiership Ambitions

The Blues team in 1997. From left to right, back row: Neil McDonald (physiotherapist), Paul Furlong, Dele Adebola, Chris Holland, Kevin Poole, Ian Bennett, Darren Purse, Michael Johnson, Martin O'Connor, Ian Bowyer (reserve team manager). Middle row: Arvel Lowe (fitness coach), Steve Robinson, Bryan Hughes, Peter Ndlovu, Nicky Forster, Jerry Gill, Jonathan Bass, Martin Grainger, Frank Barlow (assistant manager). Front row: Tony Hey, Jon McCarthy, Simon Charlton, Trevor Francis (manager), Mick Mills (assistant manager), Gary Ablett, Darren Wassall, Chris Marsden.

Ricky Otto was a positive left-winger who joined Blues from Southend United for £800,000 in the summer of 1993. He remained at St Andrew's for five years during which time he helped Blues win promotion from Division Two and also carry off the Auto Windscreen Shield at Wembley. He scored 8 times in his 62 outings for Blues before leaving the club in 1998. Otto, easily recognizible by his dreadlocks, also played for Leyton Orient and went on loan from Blues to Charlton Athletic, Peterborough United and Notts County.

Defender Paul Mardon started his professional career with Bristol City. He joined Blues in August 1991 after a loan spell with Doncaster Rovers. After 80 games he was transferred to nearby West Bromwich Albion for £400,000 in November 1993 but over the last two years he has been troubled by niggling injuries at The Hawthorns. Mardon has 1 Welsh cap to his credit.

Louie Donowa, seen here in action for Blues against Grimsby Town's Paul Agnew, was an out-and-out winger with pace, good ball skills and a big heart. A former England under-21 international, he has been in top-class football since 1982. Over the years he has served with Norwich City, Real Deportivo in Spain, Stoke City, Willem II in Holland, Ipswich Town, Bristol City, Blues (signed for £60,000 in August 1991), Burnley, Shrewsbury Town, Walsall, Peterborough United and Walsall (again). His Blues record was 21 goals in 158 first team appearances.

After making more than 330 first team appearances for Blues, full-back John Frain left St Andrew's for Northampton Town in 1997 and within a matter of months scored a dramatic winning goal at Wembley for the Cobblers against Swansea City in the Third Division play-off final. Born in Birmingham in 1968, he joined Blues as a junior and turned professional in 1986. He starred in the Leyland Daf Trophy victory at Wembley in 1991.

Steve Claridge also scored a dramatic Wembley goal after leaving St Andrew's. He found the net for Leicester City against Crystal Palace in the 1996 First Division play-off showdown and then grabbed another medal at the Empire Stadium when Leicester lifted the League Cup the following season. Claridge netted 42 goals in 120 games for Blues. He has also scored for Bournemouth, Aldershot, Cambridge United (two spells), Luton Town, Wolverhampton Wanderers and Portsmouth.

Blues' skipper Liam Daish lines up with his counterpart, mascots and officials at Boundary Park before a League game with Oldham Athletic in December 1995. It is a game Blues would like to forget – they lost 4-0, their heaviest defeat of the season. Daish was a Barry Fry signing from Cambridge United in 1994. He made almost 100 appearances for Blues before transferring to Coventry City in 1996.

During the game Blues' striker Kevin Francis, 6ft 7ins tall and weighing over 15 stones, was given a tough time by the Latics defenders. He cost the club £800,000 from Stockport County in January 1995 and went on to score 21 goals in 94 outings for the club before moving to Oxford United.

Above left: Trevor Francis returned to St Andrew's as manager in May 1996, some seventeen years after becoming the first £1 million footballer when he was transferred by Blues to Nottingham Forest in February 1979. *Above right:* Midfielder Martyn O'Connor played for Crystal Palace, Walsall and Peterborough United before joining Blues for £500,000 in November 1996. A workaholic in the engine-room, he passed the career milestone of 250 senior appearances in 1999. *Below left:* At 6ft 7in, striker Kevin Francis has been the tallest player ever to represent Birmingham City. He was at St Andrew's for three years from January 1995 to February 1998 and during that time scored 21 goals in 94 senior outings. He joined the club for £800,000 from Stockport County, having earlier assisted Derby County. When he left St Andrew's Francis signed for Oxford United.

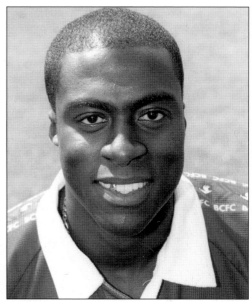

Defender Gary Ablett (left) and striker Paul Furlong (right) were team-mates at St Andrew's in the 1990s. Ablett made over 100 appearances for the club before injury forced him to miss most of the 1998/99 season and the start of the 1999/2000 season. He also played in over 100 games for both Liverpool and then Everton. Furlong started his career with Coventry City and after a spell with Watford he joined Chelsea. He switched to Blues for £1.5 million in July 1994 and has scored well over 100 goals since making his League debut in 1991.

Dele Adebola (left) at 6ft 3ins and Zimbabwean international Peter Ndlovu (right) at 5ft 8ins were united in the Blues forward line during the late 1990s and they played very successfully together. Adebola was recruited from Crewe Alexandra for £1 million in February 1998 and Ndlovu arrived from Coventry City for £1.6 million seven months earlier. Scorer of 46 goals for the Alex, Adebola netted 25 times in his first 65 games for Blues while Ndlovu, before injury struck him down early in the 1999/2000 season, had claimed a similar number of goals in almost 100 first team appearances.

Jon McCarthy breaks through his former club's defence as Blues take on Port Vale. The Northern Ireland international started his career with Hartlepool United and after playing for York City he joined the Valiants for £450,000, switching to Blues for £1.85 million in September 1997.

Steve Finnan, a Republic of Ireland 'B' and under-21 international from Limerick, joined Blues from non-League Welling United for £100,000 in June 1995. A talented winger, he made only 22 first team appearances for the club before moving to Notts County. After switching to Fulham in November 1998 he helped the Cottagers win the Second Division title in his first season with the London club.

Right-back Jonathan Bass – pictured here in action against Stoke City's striker Mike Sheron (now with Barnsley) – won England schoolboy honours before turning professional with Blues in June 1994. Over the next six years he made just over 70 first team appearances for the St Andrew's club as well as having a loan spell with Carlisle United in 1996.

In March 1997 Blues played two local derbies in a fortnight – at home to Wolverhampton Wanderers and away to West Bromwich Albion. Here are the front covers of the two matchday programmes with ex-Blues star Paul Peschisolido featured on the Albion cover (below). The home game versus Wolves attracted a crowd of almost 20,000 to St Andrew's but the Blues' supporters went home rather disappointed after seeing the visitors win 2-1.

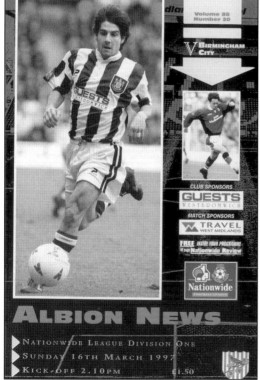

At The Hawthorns, a crowd of 16,125 saw Blues again miss out, this time losing 2-0 to the Baggies.

Blues' defenders Darren Purse and Martin Grainger challenge the Bolton Wanderers striker Dean Holdsworth for a high ball during the Nationwide League Division One game at St Andrew's in February 1999. A crowd of over 26,000 witnessed the 0-0 draw between two of the promotion chasing teams. Purse arrived at St Andrew's from Oxford United, having earlier assisted Leyton Orient; and Grainger was recruited from Brentford, having previously starred for Colchester United.